THE DIVINE LITURGY

of
Saint John Chrysostom

www.gideonhousebooks.com

The Divine Liturgy of Saint John Chrysostom

ISBN: 978-1-943133-03-1

Gideon House Books
http://www.gideonhousebooks.com

Contents

Who Was St. John Chrysostom?

John was born in Antioch in 349 to Greco-Syrian parents. Different scholars describe his mother Anthusa as a pagan or as a Christian, and his father was a high ranking military officer. John's father died soon after his birth and he was raised by his mother.

He was baptised in 368 or 373 and tonsured as a reader (one of the minor orders of the Church). As a result of his mother's influential connections in the city, John began his education under the pagan teacher Libanius. From Libanius, John acquired the skills for a career in rhetoric, as well as a love of the Greek language and literature.

As he grew older, however, he became more deeply committed to Christianity and went on to study theology under Diodore of Tarsus, founder of the re-constituted School of Antioch. According to the Christian historian Sozomen, Libanius was supposed to have said on his deathbed that John would have been his successor "if the Christians had not taken him from us".

He lived with extreme asceticism and became a hermit in about 375; he spent the next two years continually standing, scarcely sleeping, and committing the Bible to memory. As a consequence of these practices, his stomach and kidneys were permanently damaged and poor health forced him to return to Antioch.

He was ordained as a deacon in 381 by Saint Meletius of Antioch, and was ordained as a presbyter (that is, a priest) in 386 by Bishop Flavian I of Antioch. Over the course of twelve years, he gained popularity because of the eloquence of his public speaking, especially his insightful expositions of Bible passages and moral teaching. The most valuable of his works from this period are his Homilies on various books of the Bible. He emphasised charitable giving and was concerned with the spiritual and temporal needs of the poor. He also spoke out against abuse of wealth and personal property.

Do you wish to honour the body of Christ? Do not ignore him when he is naked. Do not pay him homage in the temple clad in silk, only then to neglect him outside where he is cold and ill-clad. He who said: "This is my body" is the same who said: "You saw me hungry and you gave me no food", and "Whatever you did to the least of my brothers you did also to me"... What good is it if the Eucharistic table is overloaded with golden chalices when your brother is dying of hunger? Start by satisfying his hunger and then with what is left you may adorn the altar as well.

His straightforward understanding of the Scriptures – in contrast to the Alexandrian tendency towards allegorical interpretation – meant that the themes of his talks were practical, explaining the Bible's application to everyday life. Such straightforward preaching helped Chrysostom to garner popular support. He founded a series of hospitals in Constantinople to care for the poor.

One incident that happened during his service in Antioch illustrates the influence of his sermons. When Chrysostom arrived in Antioch, the bishop of the city had to intervene with Emperor Theodosius I on behalf of citizens who had gone on a rampage mutilating statues of the Emperor and his family. During the weeks of Lent in 387, John preached twenty-one sermons in which he entreated the people to see the error of their ways. These made a lasting impression on the general population of the city: many pagans converted to Christianity as a result of the sermons. As a result, Theodosius' vengeance was not as severe as it might have been.

A sculpture of John Chrysostom in Saint Patrick's Cathedral, New York City

In 398, John was requested, against his will, to take the position of Archbishop of Constantinople. He deplored the fact that Imperial court protocol would now assign to him access to privileges greater than the highest state officials.

During his time as Archbishop he adamantly refused to host lavish social gatherings, which made him popular with the common people, but unpopular with wealthy citizens and the clergy. His reforms of the clergy were also unpopular with these groups. He told visiting regional preachers to return to the churches they were meant to be serving—without any payout.

His time in Constantinople was more tumultuous than his time in Antioch. Theophilus, the Patriarch of Alexandria, wanted to bring Constantinople under his sway and opposed John's appointment to Constantinople. Being an opponent of Origen's teachings, he accused John of being too partial to the teachings of that theologian.

Theophilus had disciplined four Egyptian monks (known as "the tall brothers") over their support of Origen's teachings. They fled to and were welcomed by John. He made another enemy in Aelia Eudoxia, the wife of the eastern Emperor Arcadius, who assumed (perhaps with justification) that his denunciations of extravagance in feminine dress were aimed at herself.

Depending on one's outlook, John was either tactless or fearless when denouncing offences in high places. An alliance was soon formed against him by Eudoxia, Theophilus and others of his enemies. They held a synod in 403 (the Synod of the Oak) to charge John, in which his connection to Origen was used against him. It resulted in his deposition and banishment.

He was called back by Arcadius almost immediately, as the people became "tumultuous" over his departure. There was also an earthquake the night of his arrest, which Eudoxia took for a sign of God's anger, prompting her to ask Arcadius for John's reinstatement.

Peace was short-lived. A silver statue of Eudoxia was erected in the Augustaion, near his cathedral. John denounced the dedication ceremonies. He spoke against her in harsh terms: "Again Herodias raves; again she is troubled; she dances again; and again desires to receive John's head in a charger," an allusion to the events surrounding the death of John the Baptist. Once again he was banished, this time to the Caucasus in Armenia.

Pope Innocent I protested at this banishment, but to no avail. Innocent sent a delegation to intercede on behalf of John in 405. It was led by Gaudentius of Brescia; Gaudentius and his companions, two bishops, encountered many difficulties and never reached their goal of entering

Constantinople.

John wrote letters which still held great influence in Constantinople. As a result of this, he was further exiled to Pitiunt (in modern Georgia) where his tomb is a shrine for pilgrims. He never reached this destination, as he died during the journey. His last words are said to have been, "δόξα τῷ θεῷ πάντων ἕνεκεν" (Glory be to God for all things).

John came to be venerated as a saint soon after his death. His disciple, Saint Proclus, Patriarch of Constantinople (434-447), during services in the Church of Hagia Sophia, preached a sermon praising his teacher. He said, "O John, your life was filled with sorrow, but your death was glorious. Your grave is blessed and reward is great, by the grace and mercy of our Lord Jesus Christ O graced one, having conquered the bounds of time and place! Love has conquered space, unforgetting memory has annihilated the limits, and place does not hinder the miracles of the saint."

This sermon helped to mobilize public opinion, and the patriarch received permission from the emperor to return Chrysostom's relics to Constantinople, where they were enshrined in the Church of the Holy Apostles.

The Eastern Orthodox Church commemorates him as a "Great Ecumenical Teacher", together with Basil the Great and Gregory the Theologian. These three saints, in addition to having their own individual commemorations throughout the year, are commemorated together on 30 January, a feast known as the Synaxis of the Three Hierarchs.

There are several feast days dedicated to him:
27 January, Translation of the relics of St John Chrysostom from Comana to Constantinople
30 January, Synaxis of the Three Great Hierarchs
14 September, Repose of St John Chrysostom
13 November, St John Chrysostom the Archbishop of Constantinople

As Taken From Wikipedia, June 2011: http://en.wikipedia.org/wiki/John_Chrysostom

About the Liturgy

The Divine Liturgy of Saint John Chrysostom is the most celebrated Divine Liturgy in the Byzantine Rite. It is named after the anaphora with the same name which is its core part and it is attributed to Saint John Chrysostom, Archbishop of Constantinople in the 5th century.

It reflects the work of the Cappadocian Fathers to both combat heresy and define Trinitarian theology for the Christian Church. The Liturgy of St. John Chrysostom was probably the divine liturgy used originally by the School of Antioch and was, therefore, most likely developed from West Syrian liturgical rites. In Constantinople, it was refined and beautified under John's guidance as Patriarch of Constantinople, (398-404). Having become the liturgical form of the Church of Holy Wisdom, Hagia Sophia, it became over time the normative liturgical form in the churches within the Byzantine Empire. The two liturgical rites of St. John Chrysostom and St. Basil in the Eastern Church became the norm by the end of the reign of Justinian.

As Taken From Wikipedia, June 2011: http://en.wikipedia.org/wiki/Divine_Liturgy_of_St._John_Chrysostom

The Great Litany and the Antiphons

Priest: Blessed is the kingdom of the Father and the Son and the Holy Spirit, now and forever and to the ages of ages.

People: Amen.

Deacon: In peace let us pray to the Lord.

People: Lord, have mercy.

Deacon: For the peace of God and the salvation of our souls, let us pray to the Lord.

People: Lord, have mercy.

Deacon: For peace of the whole world, for the stability of the holy churches of God, and for the unity of all, let us pray to the Lord.

People: Lord, have mercy.

Deacon: For this holy house and for those who enter it with faith, reverence, and the fear of God, let us pray to the Lord.

People: Lord, have mercy.

Deacon: For our Archbishop (Name), our Bishop (Name), the honorable presbyters, the deacons in the service of Christ, and all the clergy and laity, let us pray to the Lord.

People: Lord, have mercy.

Deacon: For our country, the president, and all those in public service, let us pray to the Lord.

People: Lord, have mercy.

Deacon: For this parish and city, for every city and country, and for the faithful who live in them, let us pray to the Lord.

People: Lord, have mercy.

Deacon: For favorable weather, an abundance of the fruits of the earth, and temperate seasons, let us pray to the Lord.

People: Lord, have mercy.

Deacon: For travelers by land, sea, and air, for the sick, the suffering, the captives, and for their salvation, let us pray to the Lord.

People: Lord, have mercy.

Deacon: For our deliverance from all affliction, wrath, danger, and distress, let us pray to the Lord.

People: Lord, have mercy.

Priest: Help us, save us, have mercy upon us, and protect us, O God, by

Your grace.

People: Lord, have mercy.

Deacon: Remembering our most holy, pure, blessed, and glorious Lady, the Theotokos and ever virgin Mary, with all the saints, let us commit ourselves and one another and our whole life to Christ our God.

People: To You, O Lord.

Priest *(in a low voice)*: Lord, our God, whose power is beyond compare, and glory is beyond understanding; whose mercy is boundless, and love for us is ineffable; look upon us and upon this holy house in Your compassion. Grant to us and to those who pray with us Your abundant mercy.

Priest: For to You belong all glory, honor, and worship to the Father and the Son and the Holy Spirit, now and forever and to the ages of ages.

People: Amen.

The First Antiphon

(The designated verses from the Psalms are sung with the hymn:)

People: By the intercessions of the Theotokos, Savior, save us (3).

Deacon: In peace let us again pray to the Lord.

People: Lord, have mercy.

Deacon: Help us, save us, have mercy upon us, and protect us, O God, by Your grace.

People: Lord, have mercy.

Deacon: Remembering our most holy, pure, blessed, and glorious Lady, the Theotokos and ever virgin Mary, with all the saints, let us commit ourselves and one another and our whole life to Christ our God.

People: To You, O Lord.

Priest *(in a low voice)*: Lord, our God, save Your people and bless Your inheritance; protect the whole body of Your Church; sanctify those who love the beauty of Your house; glorify them in return by Your divine power; and do not forsake us who hope in You.

Priest: For Yours is the dominion, the kingdom, the power, and the glory of the Father and the Son and the Holy Spirit, now and forever and to the ages of ages.

People: Amen.

The Second Antiphon

(The designated verses from the Psalms are sung with the hymn:)

People: Save us, O Son of God, (who rose from the dead), to You we sing: Alleluia (3).
Glory to the Father and the Son and the Holy Spirit, now and forever and to the ages of ages. Amen.

Only begotten Son and Word of God, although immortal You humbled Yourself for our salvation, taking flesh from the holy Theotokos and ever virgin Mary and, without change, becoming man. Christ, our God, You were crucified but conquered death by death. You are one of the Holy Trinity, glorified with the Father and the Holy Spirit - save us.

Deacon: In peace let us again pray to the Lord.

People: Lord, have mercy.

Deacon: Help us, save us, have mercy upon us, and protect us, O God, by Your grace.

People: Lord, have mercy.

Deacon: Remembering our most holy, pure, blessed, and glorious Lady, the Theotokos and ever virgin Mary, with all the saints, let us commit ourselves and one another and our whole life to Christ our God.

People: To You, O Lord.

Priest *(in a low voice)*: Lord, You have given us grace to offer these common prayers with one heart. You have promised to grant the requests of two or three gathered in Your name. Fulfill now the petitions of Your servants for our benefit, giving us the knowledge of Your truth in this world, and granting us eternal life in the world to come.

Priest: For You are a good and loving God, and to You we give glory, to the Father and the Son and the Holy Spirit, now and forever and to the ages of ages.

People: Amen.

The Third Antiphon

(The designated verses of the Psalms are sung with the Apolytikion.)

The Entrance

(While the Apolytikion is sung, the priest carrying the holy Gospel Book comes in procession before the Beautiful Gate and prays in a low voice:)

Priest: Master and Lord our God, You have established in heaven the orders and hosts of angels and archangels to minister to Your glory. Grant that the holy angels may enter with us that together we may serve and glorify Your goodness. For to You belong all glory, honor, and worship to the Father and the Son and the Holy Spirit, now and forever and to the ages of ages. Amen.

(The priest blesses the entrance saying in a low voice:)

Blessed is the entrance of Your saints always, now and forever and to the ages of ages. Amen.

(He then raises the holy Gospel Book and says:)

Priest (Deacon): Wisdom. Let us be attentive.

People: Come, let us worship and bow before Christ. Save us, O Son of God who rose from the dead, to You we sing: Alleluia.

(The priest enters the sanctuary. The Apolytikion is repeated and the Troparion of the church and the Kontakion of the day are sung.)

The Trisagion Hymn

Deacon: Let us pray to the Lord.

People: Lord, have mercy.

Priest (*in a low voice*): Holy God, You dwell among Your saints. You are praised by the Seraphim with the thrice holy hymn and glorified by the Cherubim and worshiped by all the heavenly powers. You have brought all things out of nothing into being. You have created man and woman in Your image and likeness and adorned them with all the gifts of Your grace. You give wisdom and understanding to the supplicant and do not overlook the sinner but have established repentance as the way of salvation. You have enabled us, Your lowly and unworthy servants, to stand at this hour before the glory of Your holy altar and to offer to You due worship and praise. Master, accept the thrice holy hymn also from the lips of us sinners and visit us in Your goodness. Forgive our voluntary and involuntary transgressions, sanctify our souls and bodies, and grant that we may worship and serve You in holiness all the days of our lives, by the intercessions of the holy Theotokos and of all the saints who have pleased You throughout the ages.

Priest: For You are holy, our God, and to You we give glory, to the Father and the Son and the Holy Spirit, now and forever...

Deacon: ...and to the ages of ages.

People: Amen. Holy God, Holy Mighty, Holy Immortal, have mercy on us (3). Glory to the Father and to the Son and to the Holy Spirit, now and forever and to the ages of ages.

Amen. Holy Immortal, have mercy on us.

Deacon: Again, fervently.

Priest *(turning towards the Prothesis, the priest says in a low voice:)*: Blessed is He who comes in the name of the Lord.

(Then turning towards the holy Table, he says:)

Blessed are You on the throne of glory of Your kingdom, seated upon the Cherubim, now and forever and to the ages of ages. Amen.

People: Holy God, Holy Mighty, Holy Immortal, have mercy on us.

The Readings

The Epistle

Priest: Let us be attentive.

(The Reader reads the verses from the Psalms.)

Deacon: Wisdom.

Reader: The reading is from (The name of the book of the New Testament from which the Apostolic reading is taken).

Deacon: Let us be attentive.

(The Reader reads the designated Apostolic pericope.)

Priest: Peace be with you.

People: Alleluia. Alleluia. Alleluia.

Priest *(in a low voice)*: Shine within our hearts, loving Master, the pure light of Your divine knowledge and open the eyes of our minds that we may comprehend the message of your Gospel. Instill in us, also, reverence for Your blessed commandments, so that having conquered sinful desires, we may pursue a spiritual life, thinking and doing all those things that are pleasing to You. For You, Christ our God, are the light of our souls and bodies, and to You we give glory together with Your Father who is without beginning and Your all holy, good, and life giving Spirit, now and forever and to the ages of ages. Amen.

The Holy Gospel

Priest: Wisdom. Arise. Let us hear the holy Gospel. Peace be with all.

People: And with your spirit.

Deacon: The reading is from the holy Gospel according to (Name). Let us be attentive.

People: Glory to You, O Lord, glory to You.

(The Deacon reads the designated pericope of the holy Gospel.)

People: Glory to You, O Lord, glory to You.

The Homily

(Following the readings, it is customary for the priest to proclaim the Gospel.)

Litany of Fervent Supplication

Priest: Let us say with all our soul and with all our mind, let us say:

People: Lord, have mercy. (once)

Priest: O Lord Almighty, the God of our Fathers, we beseech Thee, hear us and have mercy.

People: Lord, have mercy. (once)

Priest: Have mercy upon us, O God, according to Thy great goodness, we beseech Thee, hear us and have mercy.

People: Lord, have mercy. (three times)

Priest: Furthermore we pray for this country, its ruler, (title and name of the ruler), its people, civil authorities and armed forces.

People: Lord, have mercy. (three times)

Priest: Furthermore we pray for our Most Reverend Bishop (name of the diocesan bishop, or, if he be an archbishop or metropolitan, mention his rank and name), and for all the Orthodox bishops.

People: Lord, have mercy. (three times)

Priest: Furthermore we pray for our brethren: priests, deacons, monks and all other clergy, and for all our brethren in Christ.

People: Lord, have mercy. (three times)

Priest: Furthermore we pray for the blessed ever-memorable and most holy Orthodox patriarchs, for devout kings and right believing queens, for the blessed founders of this holy church and for all our Orthodox fathers, brethren, and sisters departed from this life before us, and who rest in peace here and everywhere.

People: Lord, have mercy. (three times)

Priest: Furthermore we pray for mercy, life, peace, health, salvation, visitation, forgiveness and remission of the sins of the servants of God: benefactors, trustees, members and supporters of this holy church.

People: Lord, have mercy. (three times)
(Here special petitions for the recovery of the sick, or any special needs for individual parishoners are offered.)

Priest: Furthermore we pray for those who bring offerings and do good works in this holy and all-venerable church; for those who labor in its service, for the singers and for the people here present, who await from Thee great and abundant mercy.

People: Lord, have mercy. (three times)

Priest *(in a low voice)*: O Lord our God, accept this fervent supplication from Thy servants, and have mercy upon us according to the multitude of Thy mercies; and send forth Thy compassion upon us and upon all Thy people, who await the rich mercy that cometh from Thee.

Priest: For Thou art a merciful God and lovest mankind, and unto Thee we ascribe glory to the Father, and to the Son, and to the Holy Spirit, now and ever, and unto ages of ages.

Litany for the Deceased

(This litany is offered only if there are remembrances for the deceased.)

Priest: Have mercy upon us, O God, according to Thy great mercy, we beseech Thee: hear us, and have mercy.

People: Lord, have mercy. (three times)

Priest: Furthermore we pray for the repose of the soul(s) of the servant(s) of God (name-s of the deceased), departed from this life, and that Thou wilt pardon all his (or her or their) sins, both voluntary and involuntary.

People: Lord, have mercy. (three times)

Priest: That the Lord God will establish his (or her or their) soul(s) where the just repose.

People: Lord, have mercy. (three times)

Priest: The mercies of God, the Kingdom of Heaven, and the remission of his (or her or their) sins, we ask of Christ, or King Immortal and our God.

People: Grant this, O Lord.

Priest: Let us pray to the Lord.

People: Lord, have mercy. (one time)

Priest: O God of spirits, and of all flesh, Who hast trampled down death by death, and overthrown the Devil, and hast bestowed life upon Thy world: do Thou Thyself, O Lord, grant rest to the soul(s) of Thy departed servant(s), (name-s of the deceased), in a place of brightness, a place of verdure, a place of repose, whence all sickness, sorrow and sighing have fled away. As the gracious God, Who lovest mankind, pardon every transgression which he (or she or they) has (or have) committed, whether by word, or deed, or thought. For Thou alone art without sin, and Thy righteousness is to all eternity, and Thy word is truth. For Thou art the Resurrection, and the Life, and the Repose of Thy departed servant(s) (name-s of the deceased). O Christ our God, and unto Thee we ascribe glory, together with Thy Father, Who is from everlasting, and Thine All-Holy, and Good and Life-Giving Spirit, now and ever, and unto ages of ages.

People: Amen.

Prayer of the Catechumens

(During the litany of the catechumens, the priest unfolds on the altar table the corporal [antimins], a cloth with a depiction of the burial of Christ.)

Priest: Pray unto the Lord, ye catechumens.

People: Lord, have mercy.

Priest: Ye faithful, pray ye for the catechumens, that the Lord may have mercy upon them.

People: Lord, have mercy.

Priest: That He may teach them the word of truth;

People: Lord, have mercy.

Priest: That He may reveal to them the Gospel of righteousness.

People: Lord, have mercy.

Priest: That He may unite them unto His Holy, Universal, and Apostolic Church;

People: Lord, have mercy.

Priest: Save them, have mercy upon them, preserve them, and protect them, O God, by Thy grace.

People: Lord, have mercy.

Priest: Bow your heads unto the Lord, ye catechumens.

People: To Thee, O Lord.

Priest *(in a low voice)*: O Lord, our God, Who dwellest on high and regardest the humble of heart; Who hast sent forth as the salvation of mankind Thine Only-begotten Son and God, our Lord Jesus Christ; look down upon Thy servants, the catechumens, who have bowed their heads before Thee; make them worthy in due season of the laver of regeneration. Unite them to thy Holy, Universal and Apostolic Church, and number them with Thy chosen flock.

Priest: That they also with us may glorify Thy most honorable and majestic Name of the Father, and of the Son and of the Holy Spirit, now and ever and unto ages of ages.

People: Lord, have mercy.

Dismissal of the Catechumens

Priest: All ye catechumens, depart! Depart, ye catechumens! All ye that are catechumens, depart! Let no catechumens remain! But let us who are of the faithful, again and again, in peace pray to the Lord.

People: Lord, have mercy.

Priest *(in a low voice)*: We give thanks unto Thee, O Lord God of the Powers, Who hast accounted us worthy to stand even now before Thy holy altar, and to prostrate ourselves before Thy compassion for our sins and errors of the people. Accept our supplications, O God; make us worthy to offer unto Thee prayers and supplications, and bloodless sacrifices for all Thy people. And enable us, whom Thou hast appointed in this Thy ministry, by the power of Thy Holy Spirit, blamelessly and without offense, in the pure testimony of our conscience, to call upon Thee at all times and in every place; that hearing us, Thou mayest show mercy upon us according to the multitude of Thy goodness.

Priest: Help us, save us have mercy upon us and protect us, O god, by Thy grace.

People: Lord, have mercy.

Priest: For unto Thee are due all glory, honor, and worship, to the Father, and to the Son and to the Holy Spirit, now and ever, and unto ages of ages.

People: Amen.

Prayer of the Faithful

Priest *(in a low voice)*: Again, we bow before You and pray to You, O good and loving God. Hear our supplication: cleanse our souls and bodies from every defilement of flesh and spirit, and grant that we may stand before Your holy altar without blame or condemnation. Grant also, O God, progress in life, faith, and spiritual discernment to the faithful who pray with us, so that they may always worship You with reverence and love, partake of Your Holy Mysteries without blame or condemnation, and become worthy of Your heavenly kingdom.

Priest: And grant that always guarded by Your power we may give glory to You, the Father and the Son and the Holy Spirit, now and forever and to the ages of ages.

People: Amen.

The Great Entrance

People: We who mystically represent the Cherubim sing the thrice holy hymn to the life giving Trinity. Let us set aside all the cares of life that we may receive the King of all...

Priest (*While the Cherubic Hymn is being sung, the priest prays in a low voice*): No one bound by worldly desires and pleasures is worthy to approach, draw near or minister to You, the King of glory. To serve You is great and awesome even for the heavenly powers. But because of Your ineffable and immeasurable love for us, You became man without alteration or change. You have served as our High Priest, and as Lord of all, and have entrusted to us the celebration of this liturgical sacrifice without the shedding of blood. For You alone, Lord our God, rule over all things in heaven and on earth. You are seated on the throne of the Cherubim, the Lord of the Seraphim and the King of Israel. You alone are holy and dwell among Your saints. You alone are good and ready to hear. Therefore, I implore You, look upon me, Your sinful and unworthy servant, and cleanse my soul and heart from evil consciousness. Enable me by the power of Your Holy Spirit so that, vested with the grace of priesthood, I may stand before Your holy Table and celebrate the mystery of Your holy and pure Body and Your precious Blood. To You I come with bowed head and pray: do not turn Your face away from me or reject me from among Your children, but make me, Your sinful and unworthy servant, worthy to offer to You these gifts.

For You, Christ our God, are the Offerer and the Offered, the One who receives and is distributed, and to You we give glory, together with Your eternal Father and Your holy, good and life giving Spirit, now and forever and to the ages of ages. Amen.

(The priest censes and recites in a low voice:)

Priest: We who mystically represent the Cherubim sing the thrice holy hymn to the life giving Trinity. Let us set aside all the cares of life that we may receive the King of all...

(On Sundays)

Having beheld the resurrection of Christ, let us worship the holy Lord Jesus, the only Sinless One. We venerate Your cross, O Christ, and we praise and glorify Your holy resurrection. You are our God. We know no other than You, and we call upon Your name. Come, all faithful, let us venerate the holy resurrection of Christ. For behold, through the cross joy has come to all the world. Blessing the Lord always, let us praise His resurrection. For enduring the cross for us, he destroyed death by death.

Have mercy upon me, O God, according to Your great mercy; and according to the multitude of Your compassion, blot out my transgression. Wash me thoroughly from my iniquity, and cleanse me from my sin. For I acknowledge my iniquity, and my sin is ever before me. Against You, You only, have I sinned, and done evil in Your sight, that You may be found just when You speak, and victorious when You are judged. For behold, I was conceived in iniquity, and in sin my mother bore me. For behold, You have loved truth; You have made known to me the secret and hidden thing of Your wisdom. you shall sprinkle me with hyssop, and I shall be made clean; You shall wash me, and I shall be whiter than snow. Make me to hear joy and gladness, that the afflicted bones may rejoice. Turn Your face away from my sins, and blot out all my iniquities. Create in me a clean heart, O God, and renew a steadfast spirit within me. Cast me not away from Your presence, and take not Your Holy Spirit from me. Restore to me the joy of Your salvation, and establish me with Your governing Spirit. I shall teach transgressors Your ways, and the ungodly shall turn back to You. Deliver me from bloodguiltiness, O God, the God of my salvation, and my tongue shall joyfully declare Your righteousness. Lord, open my lips, and my mouth shall proclaim Your praise. For if You had desired sacrifice, I would give it; You do not delight in burnt offerings. A sacrifice to God is a broken spirit; God will not despise a broken and a humbled heart. Do good in Your good pleasure to Sion; and let the walls of Jerusalem be built. Then You shall be pleased with a sacrifice of righteousness, with oblation and whole burnt offerings. Then they shall offer bulls on Your altar.

(Then the Great Entrance takes place.)

Deacon: May the Lord God remember all of you in His kingdom, now and forever and to the ages of ages.

People: Amen.

(The priest enters the sanctuary, while the people sing the end of the Cherubic Hymn.)

People: ...invisibly escorted by the angelic hosts. Alleluia. Alleluia. Alleluia.

(After placing the holy gifts on the holy Table, he says:)

The Petitions

Deacon: Let us complete our prayer to the Lord.

People: Lord have mercy.

Deacon: For the precious gifts here presented, let us pray to the Lord.

People: Lord have mercy.

Deacon: For this holy house and for those who enter it with faith, reverence, and the fear of God, let us pray to the Lord.

People: Lord have mercy.

Deacon: For our deliverance from all affliction, wrath, danger, and distress, let us pray to the Lord.

People: Lord have mercy.

Deacon: Help us, save us, have mercy upon us, and protect us, O God, by Your grace.

People: Lord have mercy.

Deacon: For a perfect, holy, peaceful, and sinless day, let us ask the Lord.

People: Grant this, O Lord.

Deacon: For an angel of peace, a faithful guide, a guardian of our souls and bodies, let us ask the Lord.

People: Grant this, O Lord.

Deacon: For forgiveness and remission of our sins and transgressions, let us ask the Lord.

People: Grant this, O Lord.

Deacon: For all that is good and beneficial to our souls, and for peace in the world, let us ask the Lord.

People: Grant this, O Lord.

Deacon: For the completion of our lives in peace and repentance, let us ask the Lord.

People: Grant this, O Lord.

Deacon: For a Christian end to our lives, peaceful, without shame and suffering, and for a good account before the awesome judgment seat of Christ, let us ask the Lord.

People: Grant this, O Lord.

Deacon: Remembering our most holy, pure, blessed, and glorious Lady, the Theotokos and ever virgin Mary, with all the saints, let us commit ourselves and one another and our whole life to Christ our God.

People: To You, O Lord.

The Prayer of the Proskomide

Priest (*in a low voice*): Lord, God Almighty, You alone are holy. You accept a sacrifice of praise from those who call upon You with their whole heart. Receive also the prayer of us sinners and let it reach Your holy altar. Enable us to bring before You gifts and spiritual sacrifices for our sins and for the transgressions of the people. Make us worthy to find grace in Your presence so that our sacrifice may be pleasing to You and that Your good and gracious Spirit may abide with us, with the gifts here presented, and with all Your people.

Priest: Through the mercies of Your only begotten Son with whom You are blessed, together with Your all holy, good, and life giving Spirit, now and forever and to the ages of ages.

People: Amen.

Priest: Peace be with all.

People: And with your spirit.

Deacon: Let us love one another that with one mind we may confess:

(The Priest kisses the holy Gifts saying:)

Priest: I love You, Lord, my strength. The Lord is my rock, and my fortress, and my deliverer.

(At this time it is customary for the kiss of peace to be exchanged.)

People: Father, Son, and Holy Spirit, Trinity one in essence and inseparable.

Deacon: Guard the doors. Wisdom. Let us be attentive.

The Creed

People: I believe in one God, the Father, the Almighty, Creator of heaven and earth, and of all things visible and invisible. And in one Lord, Jesus Christ, the only begotten Son of God, begotten of the Father before all ages. Light of Light, true God of true God, begotten, not created, of one essence with the Father, through whom all things were made. For us and for our salvation, He came down from heaven and was incarnate by the Holy Spirit and the Virgin Mary and became man. He was crucified for us under Pontius Pilate, and He suffered and was buried. On the third day He rose according to the Scriptures. He ascended into heaven and is seated at the right hand of the Father. He will come again in glory to judge the living and the dead. His kingdom will have no end. And in the Holy Spirit, the Lord, the Giver of Life, who proceeds from the Father, who together with the Father and the Son is worshiped and glorified, who spoke through the prophets. In one, holy, catholic, and apostolic Church. I acknowledge one baptism for the forgiveness of sins. I expect the resurrection of the dead. And the life of the age to come. Amen.

The Holy Anaphora

Deacon: Let us stand well. Let us stand in awe. Let us be attentive, that we may present the holy offering in peace.

People: Mercy and peace, a sacrifice of praise.

Priest: The grace of our Lord Jesus Christ, and the love of God the Father, and the communion of the Holy Spirit, be with all of you.

People: And with your spirit.

Priest: Let us lift up our hearts.

People: We lift them up to the Lord.

Priest: Let us give thanks to the Lord.

People: It is proper and right.

Priest (*in a low voice*): It is proper and right to sing to You, bless You, praise You, thank You and worship You in all places of Your dominion; for You are God ineffable, beyond comprehension, invisible, beyond understanding, existing forever and always the same; You and Your only begotten Son and Your Holy Spirit. You brought us into being out of nothing, and when we fell, You raised us up again. You did not cease doing everything until You led us to heaven and granted us Your kingdom to come. For all these things we thank You and Your only begotten Son and Your Holy Spirit; for all things that we know and do not know, for blessings seen and unseen that have been bestowed upon us. We also thank You for this liturgy which You are pleased to accept from our hands, even though You are surrounded by thousands of Archangels and tens of thousands of Angels, by the Cherubim and Seraphim, six-winged, many-eyed, soaring with their wings,

Priest: (Singing the victory hymn, proclaiming, crying out, and saying:)

People: Holy, holy, holy, Lord Sabaoth, heaven and earth are filled with Your glory. Hosanna in the highest. Blessed is He who comes in the name of the Lord. Hosanna to God in the highest.

Priest *(in a low voice)*: Together with these blessed powers, merciful Master, we also proclaim and say: You are holy and most holy, You and Your only begotten Son and Your Holy Spirit. You are holy and most holy, and sublime is Your glory. You so loved Your world that You gave Your only begotten Son so that whoever believes in Him should not perish, but have eternal life. He came and fulfilled the divine plan for us. On the night when He was delivered up, or rather when He gave Himself up for the life of the world, He took bread in His holy, pure, and blameless hands, gave thanks, blessed, sanctified, broke and gave it to His holy disciples and apostles, saying:

Priest: Take, eat, this is my Body which is broken for you for the forgiveness of sins.

People: Amen.

Priest (*in a low voice*): Likewise, after supper, He took the cup, saying:

Priest: Drink of it all of you; this is my Blood of the new Covenant which is shed for you and for many for the forgiveness of sins.

People: Amen.

Priest *(in a low voice)*: Remembering, therefore, this command of the Savior, and all that came to pass for our sake, the cross, the tomb, the resurrection on the third day, the ascension into heaven, the enthronement at the right hand of the Father, and the second, glorious coming,

Priest: We offer to You these gifts from Your own gifts in all and for all.

People: We praise You, we bless You, we give thanks to You, and we pray to You, Lord our God.

Priest *(in a low voice)*: Once again we offer to You this spiritual worship without the shedding of blood, and we ask, pray, and entreat You: send down Your Holy Spirit upon us and upon these gifts here presented.

And make this bread the precious Body of Your Christ.

(He blesses the holy Bread.)

Deacon *(in a low voice)*: Amen.

Priest *(in a low voice)*: And that which is in this cup the precious Blood of Your Christ.

(He blesses the holy Cup.)

Deacon *(in a low voice)*: Amen.

Priest *(in a low voice)*: Changing them by Your Holy Spirit.

(He blesses them both.)

Deacon *(in a low voice)*: Amen. Amen. Amen.

Priest *(in a low voice)*: So that they may be to those who partake of them for vigilance of soul, forgiveness of sins, communion of Your Holy Spirit, fulfillment of the kingdom of heaven, confidence before You, and not in judgment or condemnation. Again, we offer this spiritual worship for those who repose in the faith, forefathers, fathers, patriarchs, prophets, apostles, preachers, evangelists, martyrs, confessors, ascetics, and for every righteous spirit made perfect in faith.

Priest: Especially for our most holy, pure, blessed, and glorious Lady, the Theotokos and ever virgin Mary.

People: It is truly right to bless you, Theotokos, ever blessed, most pure, and mother of our God. More honorable than the Cherubim, and beyond compare more glorious than the Seraphim, without corruption you gave birth to God the Word. We magnify you, the true Theotokos.

Priest *(in a low voice)*: For Saint John the prophet, forerunner, and baptist; for the holy glorious and most honorable Apostles; for Saint(s) (Name-s), whose memory we commemorate today; and for all Your saints, through whose supplications, O God, bless us. Remember also all who have fallen asleep in the hope of resurrection unto eternal life. (Here the priest commemorates the names of the deceased.) And grant them rest, our God, where the light of Your countenance shines. Again, we ask You, Lord, remember all Orthodox bishops who rightly teach the word of Your truth, all presbyters, all deacons in the service of Christ, and every one in holy orders. We also offer to You this spiritual worship for the whole world, for the holy, catholic, and apostolic Church, and for those living in purity and holiness. And for all those in public service; permit them, Lord, to serve and govern in peace that through the faithful conduct of their duties we may live peaceful and serene lives in all piety and holiness.

Priest: Above all, remember, Lord, our Archbishop (Name) and our Bishop (Name): Grant that they may serve Your holy churches in peace. Keep them safe, honorable, and healthy for many years, rightly teaching the word of Your truth.

Deacon: Remember also, Lord, those whom each of us calls to mind and all Your people.

People: And all Your people.

Priest *(in a low voice)*: Remember, Lord, the city in which we live, every city and country, and the faithful who dwell in them. Remember, Lord, the travelers, the sick, the suffering, and the captives, granting them protection and salvation. Remember, Lord, those who do charitable work, who serve in Your holy churches, and who care for the poor. And send Your mercy upon us all.

Priest: And grant that with one voice and one heart we may glorify and praise Your most honored and majestic name, of the Father and the Son and the Holy Spirit, now and forever and to the ages of ages.

People: Amen.

Priest: The mercy of our great God and Savior Jesus Christ be with all of you.

People: And with your spirit.

Deacon: Having remembered all the saints, let us again in peace pray to the Lord.

People: Lord have mercy.

Deacon: For the precious Gifts offered and consecrated, let us pray to the Lord.

People: Lord have mercy.

Deacon: That our loving God who has received them at His holy, heavenly, and spiritual altar as an offering of spiritual fragrance, may in return send upon us divine grace and the gift of the Holy Spirit, let us pray.

People: Lord have mercy.

Deacon: Having prayed for the unity of faith and for the communion of the Holy Spirit, let us commit ourselves, and one another, and our whole life to Christ our God.

People: To You, O Lord.

Priest *(in a low voice)*: We entrust to You, loving Master, our whole life and hope, and we ask, pray, and entreat: make us worthy to partake of your heavenly and awesome Mysteries from this holy and spiritual Table with a clear conscience; for the remission of sins, forgiveness of transgressions, communion of the Holy Spirit, inheritance of the kingdom of heaven, confidence before You, and not in judgment or condemnation.

Priest: And make us worthy, Master, with confidence and without fear of condemnation, to dare call You, the heavenly God, Father, and to say:

The Lord's Prayer

People: Our Father, who art in heaven,
hallowed be Thy name.
Thy kingdom come;
Thy will be done,
on earth as it is in heaven.
Give us this day our daily bread,
and forgive us our trespasses
as we forgive those who trespass against us,
and lead us not into temptation,
but deliver us from evil.

Priest: For Yours is the kingdom and the power and the glory of the Father and the Son and the Holy Spirit, now and forever and to the ages of ages.

People: Amen.

Priest: Peace be with all.

People: And with your spirit.

Deacon: Let us bow our heads to the Lord.

People: To You, O Lord.

Priest *(in a low voice)*: We give thanks to You, invisible King. By Your infinite power You created all things and by Your great mercy You brought everything from nothing into being. Master, look down from heaven upon those who have bowed their heads before You; they have bowed not before flesh and blood but before You the awesome God. Therefore, Master, guide the course of our life for our benefit according to the need of each of us. Sail with those who sail; travel with those who travel; and heal the sick, Physician of our souls and bodies.

Priest: By the grace, mercy, and love for us of Your only begotten Son, with whom You are blessed, together with Your all holy, good, and life giving Spirit, now and forever and to the ages of ages.

People: Amen.

Priest *(in a low voice)*: Lord Jesus Christ, our God, hear us from Your holy dwelling place and from the glorious throne of Your kingdom. You are enthroned on high with the Father and are also invisibly present among us. Come and sanctify us, and let Your pure Body and precious Blood be given to us by Your mighty hand and through us to all Your people.

Deacon: Let us be attentive.

Priest: The holy Gifts for the holy people of God.

People: One is Holy, one is Lord, Jesus Christ, to the glory of God the Father. Amen.

Holy Communion

People: Praise the Lord from the heavens; praise Him in the highest. Alleluia (3).

(The Communion Hymn changes according to the Feast Day.)

Priest *(After the fraction of the sacred Bread, the priest says in a low voice)*: The Lamb of God is broken and distributed; broken but not divided. He is forever eaten yet is never consumed, but He sanctifies those who partake of Him.

(Then the priest places a portion of the sacred Bread in the Cup saying:)

The fullness of the Holy Spirit. Amen.

(He then blesses the warm water saying:)

Blessed is the fervor of Your saints, now and forever and to the ages of ages. Amen.

(Pouring the water into the Cup crosswise, he says:)

The warmth of the Holy Spirit. Amen.

(The Communion Prayers are recited silently by those prepared to receive the holy Mysteries.)

People: I believe and confess, Lord, that You are truly the Christ, the Son of the living God, who came into the world to save sinners, of whom I am the first. I also believe that this is truly Your pure Body and that this is truly Your precious Blood. Therefore, I pray to You, have mercy upon me, and forgive my transgressions, voluntary and involuntary, in word and deed, known and unknown. And make me worthy without condemnation to partake of Your pure Mysteries for the forgiveness of sins and for life eternal. Amen.

How shall I, who am unworthy, enter into the splendor of Your saints? If I dare to enter into the bridal chamber, my clothing will accuse me, since it is not a wedding garment; and being bound up, I shall be cast out by the angels. In Your love, Lord, cleanse my soul and save me.

Loving Master, Lord Jesus Christ, my God, let not these holy Gifts be to my condemnation because of my unworthiness, but for the cleansing and sanctification of soul and body and the pledge of the future life and kingdom. It is good for me to cling to God and to place in Him the hope of my salvation.

Receive me today, Son of God, as a partaker of Your mystical Supper. I will not reveal Your mystery to Your adversaries. Nor will I give You a kiss as did Judas. But as the thief I confess to You: Lord, remember me in Your kingdom.

(The priest proceeds to receive holy Communion.)

Priest *(in a low voice)*: Behold, I approach Christ, our immortal King and God.

The precious and most holy Body of our Lord, God, and Savior Jesus Christ is given to me (Name) the priest, for the forgiveness of my sins and eternal life.

(He then partakes of the sacred Bread.)

The precious and most holy Blood of our Lord, God, and Savior Jesus Christ is given to me (Name) the priest, for the forgiveness of my sins and eternal life.

(He then drinks from the holy Cup. Afterwards, he wipes the holy Cup, kisses it, and says:)

This has touched my lips, taking away my transgressions and cleansing my sins.

(The priest then transfers the remaining portions of the consecrated Bread into the holy Cup, saying:)

Having beheld the resurrection of Christ, let us worship the holy Lord Jesus, the only Sinless One. We venerate Your cross, O Christ, and we praise and glorify Your holy resurrection. You are our God. We know no other than You, and we call upon Your name. Come, all faithful, let us venerate the holy resurrection of Christ. For behold, through the cross joy has come to all the world. Blessing the Lord always, let us praise His resurrection. For enduring the cross for us, He destroyed death by death.

(The priest takes up the holy Cup, proceeds to the Royal Doors, raises the holy Cup, and says:)

Deacon: Approach with the fear of God, faith, and love.

(Those prepared come forth with reverence to receive Holy Communion while the people sing the communion hymn.)

(When administering Holy Communion, the priest says:)

Priest: The servant of God (Name) receives the Body and Blood of Christ for forgiveness of sins and eternal life.

(After Communion has been given, the priest blesses the people, saying:)

Priest: Save, O God, Your people and bless Your inheritance.

People: We have seen the true light; we have received the heavenly Spirit; we have found the true faith, worshiping the undivided Trinity, for the Trinity has saved us.

Priest *(Returning to the holy Table, the priest transfers the portions of the Theotokos and of the saints into the holy Cup. Then he does the same for those of the living and the dead saying in a low voice)*: Wash away, Lord, by Your holy Blood, the sins of all those commemorated, through the intercessions of the Theotokos and all Your saints. Amen.

Be exalted, O God, above the heavens. Let Your glory be over all the earth (3).

Priest *(the priest lifts the holy Cup and says in a low voice)*: Blessed is our God.

Priest: Always, now and forever and to the ages of ages.

People: Amen. Let our mouths be filled with Your praise, Lord, that we may sing of Your glory. You have made us worthy to partake of Your holy mysteries. Keep us in Your holiness, that all the day long we may meditate upon Your righteousness. Alleluia. Alleluia. Alleluia.

Prayer of Thanksgiving

Deacon: Let us be attentive. Having partaken of the divine, holy, pure, immortal, heavenly, life giving, and awesome Mysteries of Christ, let us worthily give thanks to the Lord.

People: Lord, have mercy.

Deacon: Help us, save us, have mercy upon us, and protect us, O God, by your grace.

People: Lord, have mercy.

Deacon: Having prayed for a perfect, holy, peaceful, and sinless day, let us commit ourselves and one another, and our whole life to Christ our God.

People: To You, O Lord.

Priest *(in a low voice)*: We thank You, loving Master, benefactor of our souls, that on this day You have made us worthy once again of Your heavenly and immortal Mysteries. Direct our ways in the right path, establish us firmly in Your fear, guard our lives, and make our endeavors safe, through the prayers and supplications of the glorious Theotokos and ever virgin Mary and of all Your saints.

Priest: For You are our sanctification and to You we give glory, to the Father and the Son and the Holy Spirit, now and forever and to the ages of ages.

People: Amen.

The Dismissal

Priest: Let us depart in peace.

Deacon: Let us pray to the Lord.

People: Lord have mercy.

Priest: Lord, bless those who praise You and sanctify those who trust in You. Save Your people and bless Your inheritance. Protect the whole body of Your Church. Sanctify those who love the beauty of Your house. Glorify them in return by Your divine power, and do not forsake us who hope in You. Grant peace to Your world, to Your churches, to the clergy, to those in public service, to the armed forces, and to all Your people. For every good and perfect gift is from above, coming from You, the Father of lights. To You we give glory, thanksgiving, and worship, to the Father and the Son and the Holy Spirit, now and forever and to the ages of ages.

People: Amen.

Blessed is the name of the Lord, both now and to the ages (3).

Priest *(The priest proceeds to the Prothesis and prays in a low voice)*: Christ our God, You are the fulfillment of the Law and the prophets. You have fulfilled all the dispensation of the Father. Fill our hearts with joy and gladness always, now and forever and to the ages of ages. Amen.

Deacon: Let us pray to the Lord.

People: Lord, have mercy (3.) Father, give the blessing.

Priest: May the blessing of the Lord and His mercy come upon you through His divine grace and love always, now and forever and to the ages of ages.

People: Amen.

Priest: Glory to You, O God, our hope, glory to You. May Christ our true God (who rose from the dead), as a good, loving, and merciful God, have mercy upon us and save us, through the intercessions of His most pure and holy Mother; the power of the precious and life-giving Cross; the protection of the honorable, bodiless powers of heaven; the supplications of the honorable, glorious, prophet, and forerunner John the Baptist; the holy, glorious, and praiseworthy apostles; the holy, glorious, and triumphant martyrs; our holy and God-bearing Fathers (name of the church); the holy and righteous ancestors Joachim and Anna; Saint (of the day) whose memory we commemorate today, and all the saints.

People: Amen. Lord, grant long life to him who blesses and sanctifies us.

Priest: Through the prayers of our holy fathers, Lord Jesus Christ, our God, have mercy on us and save us.

People: Amen.

Priest *(blessing the people)*: May the holy Trinity protect all of you.

(Distributing the antidoron, the priest says:)

Priest: May the blessing and the mercy of the Lord be with you.

Printed in Great Britain
by Amazon